Love in all forms

Jennifer Nettingham

BookLeaf
Publishing

Presentation by *BookLeaf Publishing*

Web: www.bookleafpub.com

E-mail: info@bookleafpub.com

ISBN: 9789357740418

First edition 2023

I dedicate this book to my rock Kenneth Cadogan.

My supportive parents, husband, children & friends

ACKNOWLEDGEMENT

I want to acknowledge Carol Ruark who was a huge reason i was able to complete this book, I am grateful for the time she took to proof read All my poems and offer useful feedback that allowed me to give this book to you.

PREFACE

i was inspired to do this book and challenged myself to write 21 poems in 21 days.

It has been so healing to go deep with myself and write the thoughts in my head.

Here are 18 poems from my heart to yours.

The Next What If (a panic attack in words)

I take a breath
Ok, let's go, lets do this, I'm ready.

I take a breath

slow and steady intentional and purposeful

Ok, I can do this.
Time to go.
What if, what if, what If??

So, I take a breath

short
shallow
mindless and hurried
Heart racing
I can't breathe.

Ok, just take a... what if, & what if & what if?

So, I take a breath

and I answer the question

What if Jenn?

and I take a breath

I take another breath

time to let go Jenn.

I take a breath

 I'm ok!

until...

The next What If.

Perspective

I am 5 foot 10, a lot of pounds, and I am so
very small.

I am small, compared to the billions of galaxies
and trillions of stars

The too many to count planets, moons, asteroids
and comets.

The clouds of dust & gas.

I stand outside looking up to the sky,

and i'm 5 foot 10, a lot of pounds and still so
very small.

No.

No without apologies or excuses
No without regrets
No without anger

No with certainty
No with clarity
No as a complete sentence
No
period.

Black Love

5

I am sun kissed and love my glow.

My brown skin is me,
 not a part of me,
it is who I am.

i was seven years old when i learned that this
beautiful brown skin was not beautiful to
everyone.

Finding ways to shrink my tall self, doing
whatever I could do to cover up what i always
thought was beautiful

I set out to prove that I am Not my color.

But....

that little girl grew up.

And now I respect & embrace my brown skin.

I am my color.

Proudly I say

I am Black & beautiful

I am Black & strong

I am Black & smart

I am Black & kind

and

 I am Black Love.

Where have all the nightclubs gone?

830pm

Just got paid; it's Friday night
bumpin on repeat
in my head.

Meeting my girls in an hour.

Phone Rings, Yo! what's what???
Just got paid; it's Friday night
The musics too loud, but is it really cause Just
got paid; it's Friday night

Let's go to Philly
5- Spot,
Egypt,
Filo's,
Katmandu?

I don't care where we go; I just need to dance &
we gotta hurry because the clubs close at 2.

Driving to the club, Cosmic Kev and DJ
Diamond Kuts providing the soundtrack for this
epic night.

Years pass,

Just got paid; it's Friday night
& day care closes at 6pm.

Just got paid; it's Friday night
This traffic is horrendous and day care closes at
6.

You know it's $5.00 a minute once it's past 6.

Just got paid & ugh what was the rest of that
song...
I can't remember because Yo Gabba Gabba &
Laurie Berkner are providing the soundtrack
tonight.

No energy left
humming my familiar song
Friday night..., It's 7:30 PM
Friday Night It's 8:30PM
Just got paid Frida.zzzzzzz

Texas Roller Queen

9

Waiting for the final bell to ring on Friday.

Making plans for the meet up.

Jumping off the bus, Yelling to my friend, I'll
see you at the rink...Do you need my dad to pick
you up?

The bus is pulling away but i'm not done.
Running with the bus...
Hey, who are you gonna couple skaaattteeee...
Bus gone.

Go home & wait, & wait & wait. Mom says you
want dinner? No mom $2.00 for 2 slices and a
Big Red.

2 pigtails and off I go to skate,
to group skate,
to Hokey Pokey, & to couple skate.

Noah's Umbrella Bird

The morning bell rings.
It's time for school.

Ok kiddos, sit down the teacher says.

We are going to say the alphabet and name an
animal.

I'll go first.
A- Alligator

Manisha B-Bear
The class continues listing animals and now it's
my turn.
She's getting to me Noah, L- lizard I said.

Please, oh please, let me get U next.
I've got the perfect animal.

Manisha back to you sweetie.
R-Raccoon
Miles S-Snake
Sam T-Turtle

& Noah U

Yes! it's my turn.
I got U.

I say proudly
U-Umbrella Bird

and then

Silence....

then a giggle,
then a laugh,
then my teacher says Noah i know you love
animals but you can't just make them up..

but, It's real, It's true. There is such thing as an
Umbrella Bird.

but no one listens to a 4 yr old.

Sharp Objects

razor blades
mountain pine
thistle

broken glass
porcupine quills
& needles

sharp objects cut, stick, slice & cause pain

But, what about non-physical sharp objects that
cut, stick, slice and cause pain.

a sharp wit
a sharp word
a sharp tongue
they all cut like a knife.

Love, Protection or Guidance?

Wake up and start my day

Hot coffee with the perfect amount of cream , a shower a meditation then it's time to go.

I head out the door & hear my crystals call out

 Hey, don't forget me!

How do I choose?
I need to make a decision, because
I can't walk out the house with a pocket of rocks

Do I grab the pretty pink rose quartz that promotes feelings of self-love, balances emotional health, & releases emotional blockages,

Or do I need Obsidian, a power house of protection ?

Do I need protection today?

protection from the darkness in the world or do I
need Love?

& then I remind myself that even when I need
protection,

I choose Love

Kangaroo Care

I don't know what to do.
I'm here but I am useless.

Useless as I watch the nurses take care of my
baby.

Useless as I sit while alarms and bells ring and
there is nothing I can do.

Every time an alarm goes off, I watch as my
baby's oxygen levels drop.

I watch as his heart rate decreases

& I'm useless.

I can't hold my baby.
I can't feed my baby.
I can't bathe my baby.

It feels wrong and sad and useless.

I feel a lump form in my throat and look up to
hold back my tears.

I can't be useless and weak.

I say to myself; stay strong. Don't cry.

But

I start to cry.

A gentle nurse with kind eyes says let's try
something new:

Unbutton your shirt.
I'm going to lay your baby on your chest.

I tremble with fear & with tears in my eyes.
I say I have never held him.

He's 3 months old & i've never held him.

She says it will be ok,

I will place him down.

I will arrange the cords
and you just hold him and breathe.

Hold him and breathe? I say it can't be that easy.
And she says yes, simply hold your baby and
breathe.

She lays him down and all the alarms go off. She
see's my fear and   says hold him and breathe.

I start to panic; these alarms can't be good.

She says hold him and breathe.

I'm about to cry and hand him back and all of a
sudden like magic the alarms stop ringing.

I hold him and breathe.

The numbers start climbing.

I hold him and breathe.

And for the first time in 3 months I am holding
my baby.

I sit there confused and elated and my tears of
sadness and fear are now tears of joy.
She see's the difference in my tears & says with
a wink and a smile that's what we call Kangaroo
Care.

I am holding my baby.
I'm doing kangaroo care

and

I no longer feel useless.

H2O

calming
grounding
supporting
nourishing

falling from the sky
crashing over rocks.

incredible strength
soothing

go with the flow
ride the wave.

Life Lesson every day.

Dimes

16 years of missing you
16 years of no time
16 years of thoughts of you
16 years of Dimes.

You leave them for me everyday
You put them in my path
You place them so strategically
 i can't help but laugh

Gone but never forgotten
Gone and always here
i can't help but smile when i think of you
as you show up with such tenderness & care.

16 years gone
a long long time , and like clockwork you show
up for me   and always leave a dime.

Ocean L♥ve

21

i dream of being a mermaid splashing in the
ocean blue.

Reflections of coral and splashing waves too.

i swim down deep and look up above

and all I see is an ocean of Love

Mixed messages

Breaking hearts and promises with a forked tongue of lies.

My mom always warned me about this kind of man.

A man like this can never be trusted.
A man like this will only think of himself.
This type of man is a narcissist and you need to run far, far away.

But, I love him.
I guess this is how this all works.

I don't want to love him.
He's never given me a reason to.

The more I want to forget him,
I just can't.

My mom warned me about men like this.
I just never thought that man would be my father.

Grandma's Gift

Vibrant and   fragrant

Violets were my grandma's favorite flower

When I was a little girl my job was to fill the
watering can

I would fill it and hold myself back from
running with the can by fast walking so not to
spill a drop of water

Grandma taught me how precious each drop of
water was for her flowers

She would touch the petals of each plant and
sweetly whisper a thank you before she would
water them

she taught me that violets cannot be watered
from the top

So the porous clay pot that held her beloved
plant sat inside a plastic tray

she would pour the water in the tray and again
sweetly whisper, drink up baby

I was in awe by her care of them and their care
of her

 I would watch in amazement as she
communicated with her violets and I swore they
communicated back

Grandma taught me well she showed me step by
step but i just never had grandma's special touch.

Unlike her I was cursed with a black thumb

I am happy i have this memory and blessed to
have witnessed her gift.

Moon

25

The moon big and bright
guides my path home, it shimmers
ball of light shine bright

Good Karma

I used to think karma was a scary thing,

listening to people use it as a weapon
" You just wait... Remember karma is a bi***"

But the dictionary defines karma as
the sum of a person's actions in this and previous
states of existence, viewed as deciding their fate
in future existences.

This definition gave me a new understanding

So

the next time you hear some one say what goes
around comes around

(your karma)

compliment someone
offer thanks
forgive
and show up

And just sit back and accept the karma you so
greatly deserve.

Floaters

Beta carotene
eat your carrots it will help
my eyes do not agree

Printed in the USA
CPSIA information can be obtained
at www.ICGtesting.com
LVHW020532041123
762971LV00060B/1097